Reg's Practical Guide To Understanding Computers

For Windows XP® & Windows Vista®

By Reginald T. Prior

Trademarks And Copyrights

Trademarked and or copyrighted names appear throughout this book. Rather than list and name the entities, names or companies that own the trademark and or copyright or insert a trademark or copyright symbol for with every mention of the trademarked and or copyrighted name, The publisher and the author states that it is using the names for editorial purposes only and to benefit the trademark and or copyright owner, with no intentions of infringing on the trademark and or copyrights.

Warning and Disclaimer

Every effort has been made to make this book as complete and accurate as possible. No warranties are implied. The information provided is on a "as is" basis. The author and the publisher has no liability or responsibility to any individuals or entities with any respect to any loss or damages from the information provided in this book or from the use of the utilities CD or any programs on it.

Preface

There are many books on the market that teaches people how to use their computers. But as I look through these books, I have found that they teach some of the tasks about operating their computers, but miss a lot of critical things about fully utilizing their computers. Also I found with a lot of these books are that they almost do not fully explain computer terminology at all in laymen's terms or teach people simply how to backup and restore their critical data (Documents, Pictures, etc) on their computers in case of a computer malfunction or viruses attacking their computer.

My aim of this book is to fill in these gaps in computer literacy that most books do not cover or spend sufficient time covering in common sense and in a way that is easily understood by everyone. As a computer technician for 12 years, I have come across many people that understand some things about computers, but want to have a better understanding about how they work and to fully utilize them in their everyday lives.

In this book, I will be covering both Microsoft Windows XP® and also Windows Vista® Operating Systems. At the time of the writing this book, these are the current operating systems that are installed on the majority of computers today. There are some differences between the two on where things are, but I will explain the differences for each version of Windows so that no matter which versions of Windows you have installed on your computer, you can easily follow along the with the lessons in this book.

You as the reader are the most important critics of this book. I value all of your feedback and suggestions that you may have for future books and also other things that I can do to make these books better. You can e-mail me at reginaldprior@gmail.com and please include the book title, as well as your name and e-mail address. I will review your comments and suggestions and will keep these things in mind when I write future texts. Thank you in advance,

Reginald T. Prior

Acknowledgements

This book that you are reading right now takes a lot of time and sacrifice to put together. I would first and foremost thank God for giving me at the age of six the love of working on computers that still is as strong today as it was back then. I would like to thank my wife, Sharifa for being a trooper when I was spending many hours on my laptop putting this book together and also for being there to help me read my drafts to make sure that it would be understood.

Also I would like to thank my family and many friends that helped and supported me throughout the years on many other projects and being there for me in good times and bad. I hope that you all enjoy this book as much as I had putting it together.

Chapter One: Computer Terminology Dictionary

Chapter Two: Getting Acquainted With the Desktop and Microsoft Windows®

Chapter Three: Basic Internet Browsing

Chapter Four: Using and Fully Utilizing Electronic Mail (E-Mail)

Chapter Five: The Critical Task of Backing up Your Computer

Chapter Six: Computer Maintenance and Upkeep

Chapter Seven: Taking Back Control Of Your Computer

Chapter One:

Computer Terminology Dictionary

Chapter One: Computer Terminology Dictionary

Before we go into learning how to operate Windows or Computers in general, I believe that before you can build knowledge in anything, we have to build your knowledge like a builder builds a house. First we have to have a solid foundation laid down before we can start building floors and rooms within the house. Fully understanding computer terminology and knowing what it means is like laying the foundation on the house.

Many people get confused on when they hear us geeks ask specific questions about their computer to help solve issues with their computer such as "How much RAM do you have installed on your computer" or "How much hard drive space does your computer have" either the person has no idea what we are talking about and say that this is a foreign language or the person tells the tech the hard drive space specs instead of the RAM or vice versa.

In this chapter I aim to translate what us geeks talk about when we are talking about these parts and more on a computer. Decode the foreign language so to speak. This is not a full list of computer terminology, which would be a book by itself. But this is a list of the most common terminology used for talking about things with a computer. So with no further delays, lets get started laying the foundation to being confident to speak "Computer Language".

Computer Terminology

Hardware

Hardware is the actual pieces of the computer that you can see and touch. A computer monitor is considered hardware, a computer tower or laptop is actual hardware. Printers, scanners, mouse and keyboard are considered as hardware.

Software/Programs

Software is the programs on your computer or you can buy or install that does a specific task. For example, your word processor like Microsoft Word, Excel, and PowerPoint are programs designed to create documents, spreadsheets or presentations. Microsoft's Internet Explorer® are programs designed that allows you to get onto and browse the Internet.

Microsoft Outlook are programs designed for you to create and send e-mail. Norton Antivirus, AVG and McAfee are programs designed to protect your computer from viruses and malware, which are also programs designed to try to take control your computer or worse, look for information to steal your identity among other things.

Note – You need hardware and software working together to make your computer work. Just having one without the other is like having a car with no gas in it.

Malware

Malware is software designed to take over your computer without your consent. Malware comes in many forms such as:

- Adware/Spyware – Adware/Spyware is any program that is supported by advertisements that flash within the program itself. These programs often track your internet surfing habits and cater the ads according to the types of other WebPages you visit and bombard you with pop-up ads and or e-mails about various products among other things such as changing computer settings, installing additional programs, such as key loggers, slow internet connections and Browser Hijacking which is explained next.

- Browser Hijacking – Browser hijacking is a common online attack designed to take over a computers web browser and change how and what it displays when you're surfing the Web.

- Key loggers – Key loggers are programs designed to record what you type into your computer with your keyboard. Key loggers can be used to try to track passwords and other information someone would use to go into your e-mail or online banking websites. That information can be sent back to owners of the malicious programs for identity theft or any other type of online crime.

- Toolbars – Toolbars are programs that plug into web browsers that provide enhanced functionality. Google and the Yahoo Toolbars are legitimate toolbars, but malicious toolbars can be also installed by programs that gather personal data and use that data for many online crimes.

Note – It is very important to be careful with what you or other people using your computer download and install from the Internet because it has become very easy to install these types of programs on your computer and put yourself at risk for any of the above items mentioned about viruses and malware. I will explain in detail how to protect you from these bad programs in Chapter Six: Computer Maintenance and Upkeep.

Hard Drive/Hard Disk

The hard drive is an actual part inside the computer that information is saved to. We can refer the Hard drive (Usually the C: drive in the My Computer Section) as a file cabinet that everything is stored. Inside the file cabinet are files and folders that represent our things. We would organize our files in folders so that it would be easier to pull out the things we want to see. The same thing goes in computers. Within our file cabinet, there is a folder called My Documents, My Pictures, My Music. Ideally we would create folders within these folders to identify what is inside them.

There are removable or portable hard drives which you can plug into the computer and remove from the computer for additional storage, but I would only recommend these for backup purposes. I would fully explain this and the reasons for backing up your computer in Chapter Five: The Critical Task of Backing up Your Computer.

Ram/Memory

Memory could best be described as short-term storage of the computer. It is where information is stored for short periods of time. That is why it is very important to save your work constantly just in case of a glitch happening with the computer causing it to restart or freeze up because it is only there until the computer turns off, then it is gone forever. Of course the more you have of this, the better.

The way that a computer uses the hard disk and memory to operate together can best be described as this. We remember quickly what we had done yesterday, but if we are asked about things that happened last year, we would have to think harder (Referring to our brains "Hard Drive" to remember things that happened a while ago and recall it into memory) this is how basically how information is exchanged in the computer. The computer takes information from the Hard Drive and loads it into its memory so that it could be worked with or remembered quickly.

Operating System

The operating system is the most critical piece of software for your computer. It is the "Master Program". Without it, your computer will simply not operate at all. It controls everything on your computer. It provides a mean for you to actually use your computer by providing a bridge between you and all of your installed or connected hardware. Also the Operating System is the base for the software that is installed on your system. There are several operating systems out there for computers. Microsoft Windows® is an operating system. This operating system is the focus of this book. Linux is another operating system that is available for computers. Mac®intoshes have an operating system called Mac® OS X.

Mouse

The mouse is the hardware device that is connected to your computer that looks like a flattened egg that controls the cursor on the screen. You use this device by sliding it across a "Mouse pad" or any other surface on your desk or table. The mouse has 2 buttons for clicking to perform an action. You can either "Left Click" or you can "Right Click". A picture of a mouse with which buttons are the Left or Right Click is shown below:

Cursor

A cursor is one of two things. A cursor can be an arrow ⬉ or another shaped object that moves around the screen when you move your mouse around. It acts like a pointer on the screen so that you can perform an action by Left or Right Clicking your mouse. Also a cursor can be the blinking vertical line in programs such as word processors to indicate where you are typing.

Double and Single Clicking

A Double Click is an act where you press the left side of the mouse down quickly twice without moving the mouse at all. A single click is the act of pressing down the left side of the mouse once without moving the mouse at all.

Keyboard

Keyboards are hardware devices that have different letters on keys that allow you to type.

Printer

Printers are hardware devices that perform duplication or prints.

Scanner

A Scanner is a hardware device that is connected to your computer that allows you to import items into your computer such as pictures that you have or documents that you have to save to e-mail, duplicate or archive digitally.

Icon

Icons are small pictures on your screen that can represent many things. On your desktop (The main screen on the computer), Icons can represent the programs or software that are installed on your computer. You would left double-click the picture to start and work with that particular program. Throughout this book, you will see that Icons can represent things you can do within certain programs also. Like in a word document, you can have a menu with many icons on them that can represent sending something to the printer to print to saving among many other things.

PC

This term is short for "Personal Computer". A personal computer is a computer designed to be used by one person at a time. At its core meaning, "PC" Refers to computers originally made by IBM. Nowadays, the term "PC" has been redefined considerably due to the fact that there are many companies making PC's such as Dell, HP and Toshiba to name a few.

Mac/Macintosh

This is a type of personal computer manufactured by Apple® Corporation. The Macintosh was the first computer to feature a mouse, icons and cursors to use the computer. Macintoshes are mainly used for Professional Photo, Music and Video Editing.

USB Port

The USB Ports are ports where you can plug in various devices. It is a very versatile type of connection because many hardware devices are being made to use these ports from Printers and Scanners, Digital Cameras, Flash Drives and many more things. A picture showing what a USB Port looks like is shown below.

Flash/Jump Drives

Flash/Jump drives are one of many types of removable storage. These devices are plugged into one of the USB Ports. Files, Pictures and other things can be saved to this device. These are now being used in place of floppy disks. A picture of what a Flash/Jump drive looks like is shown below.

CPU/Processor

The CPU/Processor is the "Brain" of the computer. It actually is the part of the computer that does all of the thinking for the computer.

Gigabyte

Gigabyte is a unit of computer memory or data storage capacity equal to 1,024 megabytes. The term Gigabyte can refer to both computer Hard Drives and Computer Memory. You can tell the difference about which gigabyte it is by knowing that the computer memory is always referred by the smaller number and the computer hard drive space is referred to the larger number.

Like I had stated earlier in this chapter, these computer terms or definitions are not all of the terms we talk about when we geeks discuss computers. Not by a long shot. Most other terms are out of the scope of this particular book. But the above translations of the "Computer Lingo" are all of the terminologies that you need to know to effectively be knowledgeable and comfortable operating a computer. I hope that I did not put you to sleep with all of this computer terminology and their meanings. But it is necessary to be able to follow along with the rest of this book.

The next chapter of this book goes into the fun stuff. Getting into and actually working with your computer, which is the main reason why you purchased this book! With no further delays, let's proceed to Chapter Two: Getting Acquainted with the Desktop and Microsoft Windows®.

How To Turn Your Computer On

The first thing that has to be done before we can start working with Windows is to turn your computer on. Every computer or laptop is made differently and computer manufacturers place the power button in many different places on the computer or laptop. But the one thing you need to keep in mind is that on every computer, the power button has an icon that looks like the picture below:

To turn your computer on, find the button that has the icon that looks like the picture shown above and press that button. On a desktop computer, you will find the same icon on your monitor power button also. Press the button to turn your monitor on.

How To Turn Your Computer Off (Shut Down)

To turn your computer off, you have to start a process called shutting down. The process of shutting down makes sure that the computer turns off programs and the many parts of your computer properly. To shut down your computer depends on which operating system you are using.

To Shut Down A Computer Using Windows XP:

Move your mouse cursor down to the lower left part of your screen and single left click the start menu button. It looks like this ⊞ start the start menu will come up. On the lower right part of the start menu, there will be a button that says "Shut Down" It will look like the picture shown on the next page:

Single left click on it. After you click on it, the shutdown menu will come up. Single left click the "Turn Off" button. Your computer will then shutdown and turn off by itself.

To Shut Down A Computer Using Windows Vista:

Move your mouse cursor down to the lower left part of your screen and single left click the start menu button. It looks like this ⊕ the start menu will come up. It will look like the picture shown below. On the lower right part of the start menu, there will be a button that has a right arrow symbol.

Single left click on it. After you click on it, the shutdown menu will come up. Single left click the "Shut Down" option. Your computer will then shutdown and turn off by itself.

Chapter Two:

Getting Acquainted With The Desktop And Microsoft Windows®

Chapter Two: Getting Acquainted with the Desktop
And Microsoft Windows®.

After you have setup your computer and turned it on, your computer will do a quick hardware check. After that check has completed, the computer tells the hardware to go to the hard drive and start that "Master Program" called the operating system. That process is called booting up. The booting up process basically is the act of the computer setting up everything it needs to give you the means to operate the computer at all. Once Windows has fully booted up, it will go right to the desktop screen where you can start using your computer. The pictures below are what the desktop looks like for Windows XP® and Windows Vista®.

Windows XP® Desktop

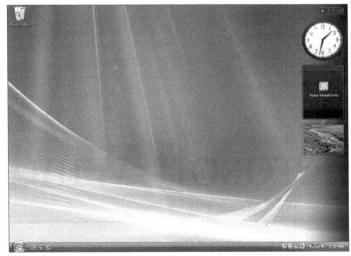

Windows Vista® Desktop

Your Windows desktop has several parts to it. The first part that we are going to talk about is located at the bottom of the desktop called the "Task Bar". The pictures on the next page show what the task bar looks like for Windows XP® and Windows Vista®. The task bar itself has several parts to it. First, we are going to talk about the Start Menu.

Windows XP® Task Bar

Windows Vista® Task Bar

The first part of the task bar that is located fully to the left side is called the start button. You notice that in the Windows XP® task bar, you have the Windows logo along with the words "Start" next to it and in the Windows Vista® task bar, it just have the Windows logo representing the start button. The start button allows us to access just about all that the computer has to offer including our programs, saved documents and pictures, and all of our computer settings. Grab your mouse and move your cursor down to the lower left part of the taskbar and single left click on the Windows logo to show the start menu.

When you single left click on the Windows logo to show the start menu, it should look like one of the following pictures below.

Windows XP® Start Menu   Windows Vista® Start Menu

At the very top part of the start menu, you will find the name of the current user that is logged in the computer. In the case of the Windows XP® screen, it is Administrator. In the Windows Vista® screen, it is VSE Test User. In the start menu, there are two areas. The left side contains three separate areas. On the top third of the left side of the menu, you have the Icons for the default programs that allow you to go to the Internet and Write E-Mail.

The middle third are icons of the programs you have been using lately. For example on the Windows XP® start menu, you have the Fax Console, Windows Media Player, Windows Messenger, and a couple of other programs. The same thing also happens in the Windows Vista® start menu also. Microsoft added this feature because it makes it convenient to have quicker access to the programs you use the most. To gain access to all of the other programs that are installed on the computer, the bottom third of the left side of the start menu has the "All Programs" option where when you single left-click on that option, a side menu will show up with all of the programs that you have installed on your computer.

On the right side of the start menu, there are icons to access different parts of Microsoft Windows® that are most used such as:

- My Documents – The default place where word processors saves files you want to keep for future retrieval

- My Pictures - The default place where image programs and or scanning software saves pictures you want to keep for future retrieval

- My Music - The default place where music programs saves music files you want to keep for future retrieval

- My Computer – My computer is where you can explore the contents of their computer drives as well as manage the files on your computer. The pictures below shows what the My Computer window looks like in Windows XP® and Windows Vista®.

Windows XP® My Computer Window

Windows Vista® My Computer Window

As you can see that in the My Computer menu, you see icons in the window that represents the hard drive (Local Disk C :), CD or DVD Drives and other things such as scanners, etc.

- Control Panel – Allows you to change settings and customize your computer.

Windows XP® Control Panel

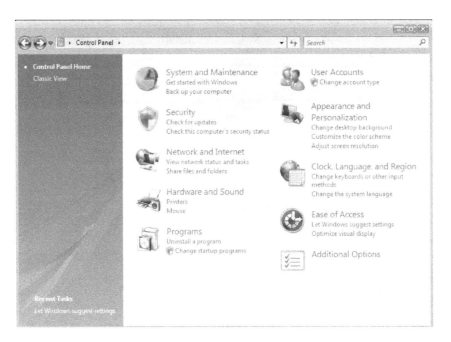

Windows Vista® Control Panel

As you can see, the Control Panel can be at first glance very intimidating because of the many options there. True there are things here that if you are not careful, that you can do some real damage to your computer. There are only a few things that we will go over in this book about the control panel due to the fact that many things in the control panel are outside the scope of this book.

What we are going to be concerned with in this book is going over how to change how your desktop looks like, setting up/changing a screen saver, adding and removing users allowed to use the computer, and adjusting the date or time on the computer. Keep in mind that when you are in doubt about anything in the control panel, don't change any settings at all. We are now going into how to change what your desktop looks like.

Changing The Background Of Your Desktop

Within the control panel, the option to change your background of your desktop is by double left clicking on the "Display" option in Windows XP® or under "Appearance and Personalization" under Windows Vista®, single left click on "Change Desktop Background". The menu that comes up should look like one of the following screens on the next page.

Note – In Windows XP®, when the display properties screen shows up, to be able to change the background of the desktop, you will have to double left click on the "Desktop" tab for the menu to show up to change the desktop background. Windows Vista® goes right to the desktop menu screen.

Windows XP® Desktop Background Menu

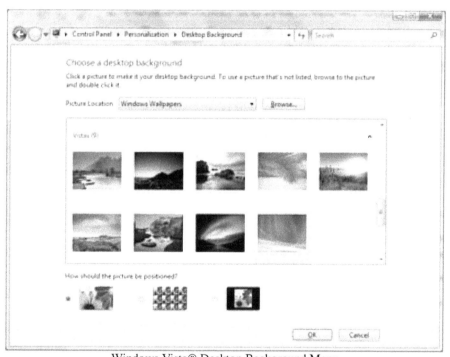

Windows Vista® Desktop Background Menu

To change the background in either Windows XP® or Windows Vista®, single left click on a picture or background pattern that is listed in the list. If you are not sure on which each picture looks like, just single left-click on it once and in the small screen above the menu, a small representation of what it would look like full screen. Once the background has been selected, you can choose how you want it to appear on the screen by choosing one of the options under the position menu in Windows XP® or on the bottom of the screen in Windows Vista® under the "How should the picture be positioned "section of the window.

Here's an explanation of the three options of how you can have the picture arranged on your desktop:

- Centered – The picture will appear in the center of the screen with the pictures real size

- Tile – The picture will appear with as many images as necessary to fill the screen shown like tiles on a kitchen floor.

- Stretch – The picture will appear once, stretching it to fill up the whole screen.

As you will notice in the area where all of the pictures are, there are more pictures there than what is shown currently. In the same area where the pictures are, you will notice off to the right what we would call "Slider Bars". Here's what they would look like.

Windows Vista® Slider Bar   Windows XP® Slider Bar

If you had wanted to see more pictures than what they initially show in the menu, you would move your mouse cursor ▶ to the middle part of the slider bar where the actual slider is and single left click and hold the button down then move your mouse up and down to show more things in the menu or single left click on the up or down arrows to move the menu up or down. In most programs or "Windows" in Windows, you will see these same sliders indicating that is more there than is showing currently.

Once the image and desired position have been selected, single left click the OK button in the menu and the desired changes will take place.

Adding/Changing Users In Windows

Do you have more than one person that will be using your computer? Do you also want to keep your documents and your other files separate from the other person that will be using your computer and vice versa? In this section, you will learn how to add/change users to Windows. Adding users is a great way to keep your personal files separate while still having the ability to share programs. The pictures shown below are from Windows XP®, but these instructions are exactly the same in Windows Vista®.

First you will need to open the Control Panel by single left clicking on the Start Button and then single left click on the Control Panel. In the Control Panel, scroll down to the Users Accounts Icon and double left click it. (note: If your control panel doesn't look like the one below you will need to click "Switch to Classic View" located on the left sidebar, and it should look like the picture shown on the next page:

With the Users Accounts window open, single left click on the "Create a New Account" option. The window should come up like the picture shown below:

Move your mouse cursor and single left click on the "add a new account" link in this menu. Enter the name of the new user in the box provided and then single left click on the next button.

Name the new account

Type a name for the new account:

New Users

This name will appear on the Welcome screen and on the Start menu.

Next, choose the account type. If you want the user to have full access to the computer, then you need to choose the Computer Administrator option. If you want the user to have limited access to the computer, meaning that the user cannot just install any kind of programs without restrictions, you should choose the limited option. I recommend using the limited option; however, most people will use the administrator option. When finished, single left click the Create Account button.

You will return to the User Accounts window and you should now see your new user's icon.

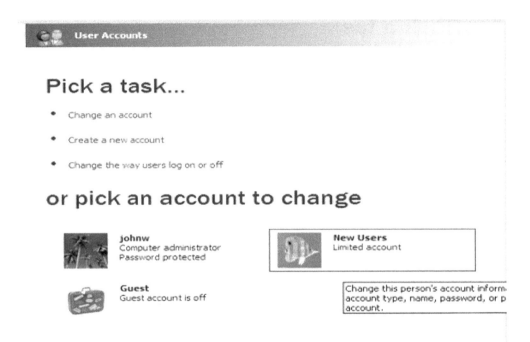

Changing User Account Type

If you want to make changes to an account that is already on this computer, move your mouse cursor to the account you want to change and single left click on it. You can change the account password among other things.

Account Type Meanings:

Administrator	Limited Account Access
This type of user has the ability to install, remove and change any of the settings on the computer, in other words, full unrestricted access to the computer.	This user can use the programs installed on the computer, but cannot change any settings. This setting is perfect for anybody outside of yourself using this computer.

Changing/Configuring Your Screensaver

When you're working on your computer and the phone rings, or any other situation happens where you have to leave your computer for some period of time. Well, back in the eighties and early nineties, people would leave their computer for a long time and have the same program on their screen. There is nothing wrong with this practice in general; as it saves time on when you have to come back to work on your computer.

But what was happening was a process was happening called "Phosphor burn-in" or just plain burn-in, which is a shadowing or ghosting of a image on the screen. You could be working on another program, but see a ghost image of the program in the screen that you or another person was looking at for long periods of time. The picture shown below shows an example of what a monitor burn-in image looks like.

Screensavers were then created to resolve this issue by showing different images on the screen to prevent monitor burn-in, in which permanently damages the monitor. To change/configure a screensaver, single left click the start menu and move your mouse cursor to control panel icon and single left click on the words control panel. In Windows XP®, you will double click on the "Display" Option and single left click on the "Screen Saver" tab up at the top of that menu. Your screen should look like the picture shown on the next page:

Note – Most new computer monitors have a "Power Save" setting that if the monitor detects no activity happening on the screen after some period of time, then the monitor shuts itself down. But if you move your mouse or do anything else on the computer, the monitor then turns itself back on.

In Windows Vista®, you would in the control panel, single left click on "Appearance And Personalization" and in that menu, select "Screen Saver". Your screen should like the following picture below:

From the drop list in either Windows XP® or Windows Vista, move your mouse cursor to the section where it says "Screen Saver" with what we call a "Drop Menu" and single left click on the down arrow to show all of the screen savers in the drop menu.

Choose one from the drop list by single left clicking on one of the choices. A small preview is shown in the small monitor screen above. If you want to see how the screensaver looks like on the screen before making it a final decision, you would single left click on the "Preview" button in the window and the screensaver comes up full screen. To get out of preview mode, just move the mouse around and it should go back to the screensaver menu.

You can modify the time the computer waits before the computer starts the screensaver by typing in a number that would represent the amount of minutes in the box below the drop menu for the selection of screensavers. When you are satisfied with choosing the screensaver and amount of time the computer waits before starting the screensaver, single left click the OK button. Now your screensaver is all setup and ready to go!

Searching For Things On Your Computer

The last section that we're going to cover from the start menu is one of the more important parts. Especially if you have a tendency to forget where things were saved is search feature. Computers today hold a great deal of information. because of this, I strongly suggest when you are working on anything on your computer that you make sure that you save them to the "My Documents", "My Pictures" or "My Music" Folders. Why do I suggest these three folders? I suggest these folders because for one, they are easily accessible from anywhere on the computer, and it makes it simpler to backup the computer.

For an example, if you were working on an important presentation and know that you had saved it on the computer, but forgot where on the computer it was saved to, the search feature can help you out . To get to the search menu so that you can search for and find that document or presentation, you would single left click the start menu and single left click on the "Search" Item on the right section of the start menu. The search page will come up like the picture shown below.

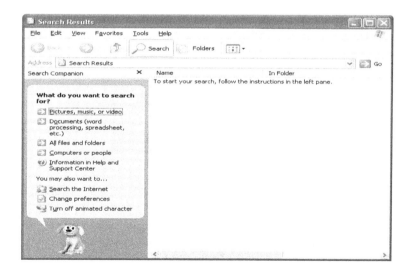

To search on your computer for documents and other things, move your mouse cursor to where it says on the left side of the search window under the "What do you want to search for" menu section and single left click on the "All files and folders" option. A window will come up with a text box where you can type in the name of the document or file that you are looking for. The picture below shows what this window should look like in Windows XP®

27

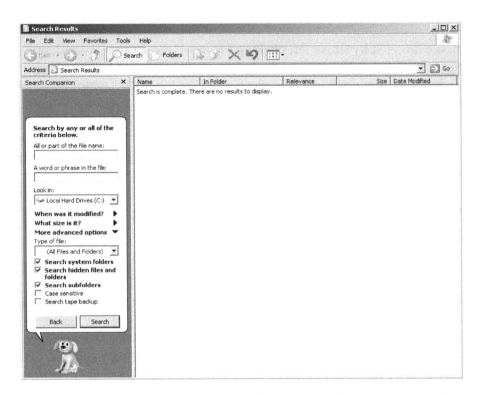

In the Section "All or part of the file name", type in the name or phrase you think that you saved the file under then move your mouse cursor to and single left click the "Search' button. The search will go through. The results will show up in the right section of the window. You can type a name or phrase in the "A word or phrase in the file" text box, but it takes an extremely long time in searching because the search is looking for the phrase you had typed in that box in <u>EVERY SINGLE FILE</u> on the computer, which takes a very long time. Only use this option if the first search does not find the file that you are looking for.

In Windows Vista®, Microsoft changed the way you search for files by integrating the search in the start menu itself. You search for files in Windows Vista® by single left clicking on the start menu, type the phrase or words you want to search for in the search box on the start menu. It looks like the picture below:

After you type in the phrase in the search box, single left click on the search button , the search will start. The search results will show in the start menu itself, as shown in the picture shown:

28

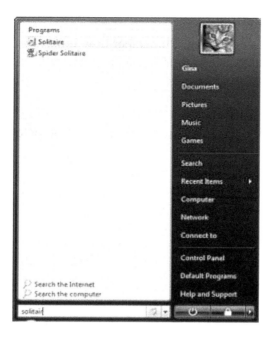

These past sections had explained the start menu and the many options grouped together. The start menu makes it easier to use your computer.

Reading Windows Pathnames

Every file on your computer has a pathname. A pathname is in short, is the exact location of a file on your computer. You might be asking yourself, how do I find the pathname of a file on my computer? Well the pathname is near the top of the current window that you have open. The picture below shows exactly where the pathname usually is located in a window.

Say for instance your budget that you typed out on a word processor is located at

C:\Documents **And Settings\User\document.doc?**

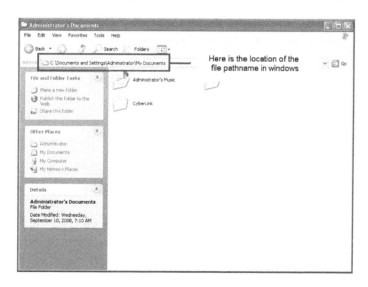

How would you decipher exactly on your computer where this file is located? Well, I am about to explain how to go straight to this document. Remember how I told you in chapter one the C: drive was like a file cabinet? And how things inside the file cabinet were organized by files inside folders? Well, files on computers are organized the same way.

First, move your mouse cursor and single left click on the start menu, then move your mouse cursor and single left click on the "My Computer" menu. Your "My Computer" window will come up. Then, move your mouse cursor to the Local Disk C: icon and double left click on it. That takes care of the C:\ part of the whole pathname. Look in that window for the "Documents And Settings" Folder. It will actually look like a folder.

Look for the User folder in that folder. Then you would double left click on that folder. Now looking in that folder, you should see the document.doc file that you are originally looking for. That's in a nutshell is how you would read a pathname.

The Shortcuts/Open Programs Area Of The Windows Toolbar

The shortcuts area is the section on the tool bar to the right of the start menu where you access particular programs quickly. The icons that usually are on the shortcuts area are:

- This shortcut represents the desktop. It minimizes all of the open Windows so that you can access a clean desktop

- This shortcut represents Microsoft's Internet Explorer®. This program is used to access the Internet

- This shortcut represents Windows Explorer. This is used to access files and folders.

Note – This section of the Shortcuts/Open Programs area are the same for Windows Vista®.

The open programs area is the section next to the shortcut area where we can see buttons that represents programs, menu items or folders that are currently open on the computer.

You go back and forth to each program simply by moving your mouse cursor to the desired program and single left clicking the desired program and whatever you were working on in that program will come back up on the screen for you.

The Notification Area Of The Windows Toolbar

The notification area of the Windows Toolbar is the icons to the far right that represent programs that starts up automatically when the computer boots up. Also displays alerts about when Microsoft releases updates to the Windows, and the current time.

Changing The Time On Your Computer

On the far right of the Windows task bar notification area, there is the clock. If you move your cursor over the clock and leave the cursor there for a couple of seconds without clicking on anything, the full date will show as a mini popup. To change the time or date on the computer, double left click on the time in Windows XP® or single left click on the clock and single left click on "Change date and time settings link in Windows Vista®, and the date and properties window will come up looking like one of the pictures shown below:

Windows XP®   Windows Vista®

In Windows XP®, to change the date, select the desired month from the drop menu by single left clicking on the down arrow next to the month menu, and select the desired month by moving your mouse cursor over the desired month and left single click on the month. The month would be selected. To change the year, move the cursor to either the up or down arrow where the year is and either single left click on the up arrow to move the year up and single left click on the down arrow to move the year down.

To change the time, move your mouse cursor over the section of time you want to change and single left click on it, type the number of the desired hour or minutes depending on which section of time you were changing. After you were done making desired changes to the date and time, single left click the "Apply" button and then single left click the "OK" button.

In Windows Vista®, single left click the "Change date and time" button and you would do essentially the same thing to change the time as you would do in Windows XP®. You can change the time zone of the computer by in Windows XP®, by single left clicking the "Time Zone" tab at the top part of this window, select the desired time zone from the drop menu and single left clicking the "Apply" and single left clicking the "OK" button. In Windows Vista®, you would single left click on the "Change time Zone" button and essentially do the same thing to change the time zone as you would do in Windows XP®.

Using The Recycle Bin

The recycle bin is space reserved on the computer so that if accidently hit the delete key and delete a file or folder, you can easily retrieve it. Deleting a file is a 2 step process on Windows. By default, the recycle bin can restore a file or folder back to the place it got deleted from. For example, if the file got deleted from the "My Documents" folder, you could easily restore it back to the my documents folder. The recycle bin keeps documents or folders there until it is permanently "emptied" from the recycle bin. Then the file or folder is gone forever.

To open the recycle bin, double left click on the recycle bin icon ![Recycle Bin icon] on the desktop. The recycle bin window will then come up looking like one of the pictures shown below:

Windows XP® Recycle Bin

Windows Vista® Recycle Bin

To put things in the recycle bin, single left click on the file or folder you want to have removed from the computer and hit the "Delete" key on the keyboard. Windows will ask you the question "Are you sure you want to send this file to the Recycle Bin?" with 2 buttons saying yes or no. If you select no, nothing happens. If you single left click yes, the files will be sent to the recycle bin.

To restore a file or folder, move your cursor to the desired file in the recycle bin to be restored; single left-click on it and single left click the "Restore the selected item" the file or folder will be taken out of the recycle bin and placed back to the place it was before on the computer.

To empty the recycle bin (Remember, after you empty the recycle bin, everything that is here is GONE FOREVER!), single left click the "Empty The Recycle Bin" button. Windows will ask you the question "Are you sure you want to delete" and with 2 buttons saying yes or no. If you select no, nothing happens. If you select yes, then the files will be deleted.

This concludes chapter two on getting to know the Windows desktop and the many features that are available in Windows. Hopefully up to this part in the book, you should feel comfortable working on your computer and explore in confidence on the other inner workings of Windows. We proceed now to Chapter Three: Basic Internet Browsing.

Chapter Three:

Basic Internet Browsing

Chapter Three: Basic Internet Browsing

The Internet is many things to many people. Some people use the Internet for things such as finding shopping deals and travel fares. Some people use the Internet for news and information. Some people use the Internet to express themselves through blogs (Online Diaries), Video Sites (YouTube) or Social Networking websites (MySpace, Face book, Twitter). And other people use the Internet for income or another way to sell things that they don't want anymore (E-Bay).

People use the Internet for malicious acts also. I will explain that in more detail in Chapter Six: Computer Maintenance and Upkeep. This chapter is concerned about getting you confident to discover the many millions of websites on the Internet and to make sense of using the Internet and using web browsers.

In chapter one, we explained what a web browser is. A web browser is a program that allows you to easily navigate the internet. So how do you get connected to the internet? Well, first and foremost, you have to sign up with an internet service provider or ISP. Your internet service provider could be your local cable or Telephone Company, or a national Wi-Fi internet carrier such as Verizon or AT&T. There are also dial-up services that you can sign up with such as AOL, but the price of high-speed internet has gone down to being very affordable and does not tie up your phone line and is dramatically faster, it will be worth getting a high speed line installed.

After you have signed up with an internet service provider and have them come out to your home and setup the service, you are ready to go. If you already have internet service, then we are ready for the next step, opening up your web browser. In Windows, you already have a web browser installed on your computer called Microsoft's Internet Explorer®.

On your desktop or your taskbar, you will find an icon that looks like this . You double left click on this logo and Microsoft's Internet Explorer® comes up and load the default website that has been programmed into the program. You can change this webpage if you like, but will go over this later in this chapter.

Microsoft Microsoft's Internet Explorer® 7

Before we go into the sections of your web browser so you can surf the internet, there is more "Computer Lingo" that describes things on the internet. Don't worry; this list is not as long as the list in chapter one talking about computers in general. These and many more terms can be found at http://www.netlingo.com.

Email -- (Electronic Mail) Messages, usually text, sent from one person to another via computer

Hyperlink / Link - The text or graphics on a Web site that can be clicked on with a mouse to take you to another website or a different area of the same Web page.

Download - To transfer a file or files from one computer to another.

E-Commerce - Simply put, it means conducting business online

Encryption - The process of protecting information as it moves from one computer to another

ISP - A company that provides user's access to the Internet.

Username- The name you use to access certain programs, Web sites, software, or networks.

Login / Log In - The act of connecting to or accessing a remote computer system, network, or server

Netiquette - The code of conduct and unofficial rules that govern online interaction and behavior

Password - A combination of letters and other symbols needed to login to a computer system.

Phishing - An online scam in which the perpetrator sends out a large number of legitimate looking e-mails that appear to come from respected companies (such as Citibank, eBay, PayPal, MSN, Amazon.com, Yahoo, Best Buy, AOL, etc.) with the intent of "fishing" for personal and financial information from the recipient. These e-mails are falsely claiming to be the respected company who needs the user's information to update their files, when in fact, it is an attempt to scam the user into surrendering private information that will later be used for identity theft.

The phony e-mail directs the user to go to a Web site with the logo of the respected company, where they are asked to update personal information (such as passwords and credit cards, social security numbers, and bank account numbers) which the legitimate organization already has. The Web site, however, is bogus and has been established only to steal the users' information. The e-mail usually includes a threat stating the user's account will close if they do not receive this updated information in a specified time period.

Search Engine - A Web site (actually a program) that acts as a card catalog for the Internet.

Webmail - Webmail allows you to access your E-Mail on a Web page, using your web browser. This means you can read, send, and organize your e-mail on any computer, anywhere in the world, with an Internet connection. Webmail for an example are services such as Gmail, yahoo, or hotmail to name a few. Your ISP can also have a webmail service so that you can look at their email from anywhere on the Internet.

So let's go over the many parts of your web browser so that you will be better able to surf the internet. The top section of the web browser contains 99% of what you will need to be able to surf the internet.

Top Part Of Microsoft's Internet Explorer® 7

The picture above with the top sections of Microsoft's Internet Explorer® 7 show that many browsers share the same features. So let get started by going over the features and exactly what they mean.

Navigate Backwards And Forward – If you are looking at multiple websites for a period of time, and you come upon a webpage that you may have wanted to look at, but quickly clicked on another link. If want to go back to look at that previous webpage, the left arrow key will take you back to the previous webpage you were looking at, and the right arrow key will take you to the webpage that you were looking at before you clicked the left arrow key.

URL Of Current Page – Address of the current page being viewed. If this box shows http://www.yahoo.com, the yahoo website should be showing below. Every webpage has a unique URL or address. You can also type in a specific webpage into this box by moving your cursor to this box and single left click on the box. It should all highlight in blue. When it is highlighted, you can type in the desired webpage you want to go to starting with www. Desired website name here .com, org, net or gov.

Reload/Stop Loading Page - When displaying a webpage, your web browser downloads the webpage from the Internet onto your computer. Therefore if the webpage changes, you can update the webpage in your browser window by clicking the **Reload button** with the green arrows. If the webpage is taking too long to load for any reason, you can stop the webpage by clicking on the **Stop button** with the red X. Click on the Reload button to start the downloading process again from the beginning.

Search Provider/Engine – This section of the web browser makes it easy to enter words to send directly to search engines. That will be discussed later in this chapter.

Return To Home Page – You click on the "Home" button to return you back to the default web page that is set for the web browser.

Bookmark/Add Current Page To Favorites – Favorites and Bookmarks are websites that you visit often to be within easy reach. If you find yourself always going to say, www.cnn.com you can "Bookmark" the webpage and go to your bookmarks menu with your mouse and single left click on the bookmark and it will then go to that particular website that you had bookmarked saving you from constantly typing it into the URL Box.

Like I said at the beginning of this chapter, there are now millions, if not billions of websites on the internet that covers any interest you may have and many other things. So how do you discover let alone find all of these WebPages? We start by typing in what we are interested in seeing on the internet by going through a search engine. A search engine collects information from all the websites on the internet and puts them into a webpage where you will be able to search and find them.

Using Search Providers/ Engines To Find Things On The Internet

There are many search engines on the internet that allows you to find websites that may interest you. The most used search engines are:

- Google – www.google.com
- Yahoo – www.yahoo.com
- MSN (Microsoft Search) – www.msn.com

The following sections in this chapter use Google search located at www.google.com . I find that Google has the most current and accurate databases of websites, and has a very simplistic layout which is easier to read as per the picture shown below:

Say for example that we were in the market to purchase a car and want to do some research on various models to make sure that we are getting not only the best deal, but we are getting the best car to suit our current needs and price range. We can search Google for a specific vehicle type or model, but in this case, we are going to type in the box "car reviews" just like it is shown in the next picture:

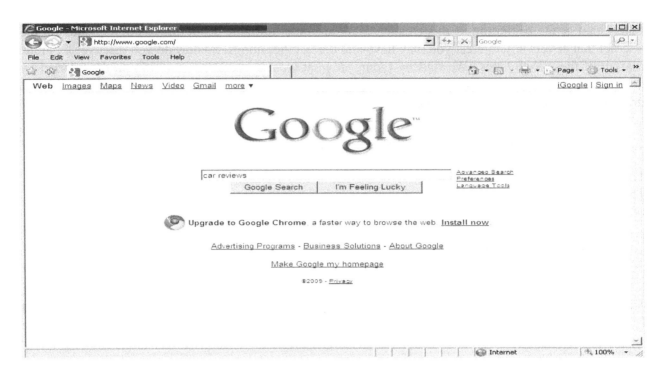

Single left click on the "Google Search" button and the results will show up like shown in the picture below:

As you can see, a lot of results came back for just the term "Car Reviews". Just a note for you to keep in mind, usually the top 20 results are exactly you are searching for. You can go deeper in the search, but usually the deeper you go into the results of a results, the less likely that the particular results show what you are looking for in the first place. Move your mouse cursor to a link (Usually in Blue Letters) and single left click on what looks interesting that you want to check out, and you will be taken to that webpage.

Well, that is how you would use a search engine to look for various things on the internet. Please feel free to try the other search engines out there if you wish. Have fun discovering the many different things on the Internet.

Adding And Using Bookmarks/Favorites

Bookmarks/Favorites are a quick & easy way to remember websites that you visit often. The instructions below show you how to create and use them.

To create favorites in Microsoft's Internet Explorer®

1. Go to the webpage you want to bookmark.
2. Single left click on the **Add to Favorites icon** or go to the **Favorites** menu.
3. Then single left click on **Add to Favorites**.
4. Give the webpage a name (e.g. *American Revolution*) or keep its original name.
5. Click **Add**.

To view and use favorites in Microsoft's Internet Explorer®

1. In Microsoft's Internet Explorer®, single left click on the **View Favorites** button and select **Favorites**. (Another option is to single left click on the **Favorites menu** in the main toolbar.)
2. From that list, single left click on the bookmark of the webpage you want to see.

In this chapter, we went over the meat and potatoes of surfing the Internet and being able to bookmark websites as we come across them. Don't be afraid to do different kinds of searches and discover things that are out there.

Changing Default Web Page When Your Web Browser Loads

When you double left click on the Microsoft's Internet Explorer® and the program loads up, the first web page that comes up is what we call the default or your home page. More than likely, the web page that comes up first is not the one that you would like to first come up when you go onto the Internet. This section shows you how to change that default or home page to whatever website you want it to be.

To change the default or home page of your web browser to the website of your choice, either it be a news website such as cnn.com or anything else, you would open up your web browser of choice and get it to the default or home page.

Microsoft's Internet Explorer® Main Menu

In Microsoft's Internet Explorer®, move your mouse cursor to the tools menu and single left click on the menu. Move your mouse cursor down to where it says Internet options and single left click on that. Then the Internet options menu should show up like the picture shown on below:

Microsoft's Internet Explorer® 7 Options Menu

In Microsoft's Internet Explorer®, move your mouse cursor to the tab at the top of the pop up window where it says "General" in the options pop up window and single left click on it. There is a text box where it says "Home Page". Erase what is in that text box and type in the web page that you wish to be the default or home page, move your mouse cursor to the "ok" button and single left click on it. Your default home page has now been set to the web page that you have typed into the home page text box.

And that is it! That is how you set the default or home page for the browser of your choice. From now on, the first web page that comes up when will be the web page of your choice and not the one that got programmed in when you the web browser got installed on your computer.

Chapter Four:

Using And Fully Utilizing Electronic Mail (E-Mail)

Chapter Four: Using and Fully Utilizing Electronic Mail (E-Mail)

Electronic Mail or E-Mail for short changed how people communicate from the business world, to families that live far away to easily stay in touch. E-Mail allows you not only to send letters to people; you can also send pictures and more recently small video clips. Many people already know how to send an e-mail, but not fully utilizing the powers of e-mail. This chapter will attempt to do that. We will like in other chapters, build your skills from the ground up.

This chapter covers Microsoft Outlook® (Microsoft Mail® for Windows Vista®). Also there are many webmail services out there like Yahoo mail, Google's Gmail, and Microsoft's Hotmail. These services also give you e-mail which gives you the distinct advantage of not tying you to just the e-mail address that your Internet Service Provider has given you and with these services, you can check and write email from any computer or device with an internet connection.

Even though these online services will not be covered in this chapter, you can follow along and the features in most cases, are the same as in Microsoft Outlook®. Before we get into working with these E-Mail Programs, we do have to setup your E-Mail program to work with the E-Mail address that your Internet Service Provider has given you to use. The 4 things we will need to get your account to work are listed below:

1. Your Internet Service POP Server addresses (POP stands for Post Office Protocol). It basically handles E-Mail that is coming in from people that has sent you E-Mail.

2. Your Internet Service SMTP Server address (SMTP stands for Simple Mail Transfer Protocol). This is used to send messages and forwards that you have written to people.

3. The username that you gave the Internet service provider to setup your Internet account with them.

4. Also we will need the password that you gave the Internet service provider to setup your Internet account with them.

If you don't remember or lost the documentation that they gave to you, you are going to have to call the customer service of the Internet Service Provider that you have to get this information, because you are going to need it to get Microsoft Outlook ® to send and receive E-Mails at all. When we have this information, we can move on to the next step: setting up the e-mail program itself.

Setting Up Your E-Mail Account On Outlook Express

To setup the e-mail account for your Internet Service Provider, we would have to start up Microsoft Outlook® and go through the setup wizard to input the information from them. First you would single left click on the start menu and single left click on the "All Programs" section of the start menu. Then a side menu pops up and you can then single left click on "Outlook Express" for Windows XP® or "Windows Mail" for Windows Vista®. They are basically the same program.

Microsoft Outlook® will start up and if it is the first time that you are starting up this program, a setup wizard starts up like in the pictures shown below. We will go step by step in setting up your e-mail account to work with Microsoft Outlook®.

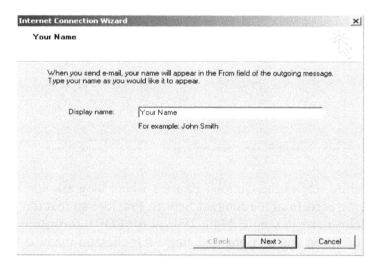

This screen is the first step in the Outlook Express wizard where they ask you to type in your name. Type in your name and single left click on the next button at the bottom of the window.

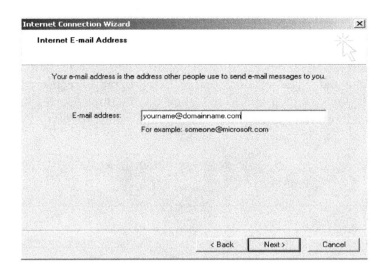

This screen is the second step in the Outlook Express wizard where they ask you to type in the e-mail address what your Internet Service Provider had given to you. It is usually username@yourinternetserviceprovidername.com, .org or .net. Type in your email address and single left click on the next button at the bottom of the window.

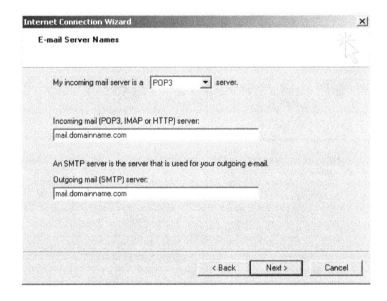

The third screen is the third step in the Outlook Express where they ask you to type in the POP and SMTP information that we need from the Internet Service Provider so that the program could connect to the right servers to deliver and to send E-Mail. Type in the POP information in the top text box and the SMTP information in the bottom text box and single left click on the next button at the bottom of the window.

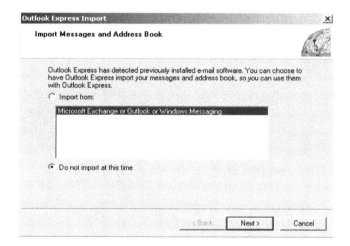

The fourth screen is the fourth step in the Outlook Express wizard where they ask you to type in your full e-mail address and the password to the account, information you gave to the Internet Service Provider when you setup internet service through them. Type in your email in the top box and your password in the bottom box and single left click on the next button at the bottom of the window.

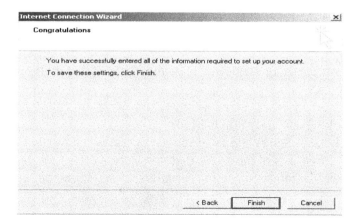

The fifth screen is the fifth step in the Outlook Express wizard where they ask you to import setting from another e-mail program. Single left click on the "Do not import at this time" circle and then single left click on the next button at the bottom of the window.

The last screen tells you that you have successfully entered all of the information that the program needs to start downloading and sending email through your Internet Service Provider's servers. You now click on the "Finish" button and then the program will finish loading. When the main screen comes up, single left click on the send/receive button in Outlook Express to download new E-Mail messages. Now we have everything setup, let's get started with fully utilizing the power that is E-Mail.

The Main Screens Of Your E-Mail Program

Windows Outlook Express/Windows Mail Main Screen

As you can see, This program is divided into three sections

- The top section of the main window shows the list of e-mails that are in your Inbox. The inbox holds messages that have been downloaded from your Internet Service Provider and e-mails that you have not checked previously or deleted.

- The lower section of the main window is called the "Preview" window. It displays the contents of the message that is currently selected from the top section window.

- The left section of the main window lists the folders that both programs sets up during configuration such as:

  1. Inbox – Holds Your Incoming E-Mails
  2. Sent/Sent Items – Stores copies of messages that you have sent to people
  3. Drafts – Stores drafts of messages that you were working on, but haven't sent yet
  4. Deleted/Deleted Items – Contains E-Mails that have been deleted

Sending E-Mails

To create a email in Outlook Express/Windows Mail, single left click on the "Create Mail" button. The button is located at the top toolbar in the program just below the file menu. A new mail message screen will pop up.

Create Mail Button In Windows Mail/Outlook Express

New Mail Message -Windows Mail/Outlook Express

To create a message you have to have the person's e-mail handy. Make sure the spelling of the e-mail is correct because your message will not be sent at all if the spelling is incorrect. The steps below are how you would compose the e-mail in either program

1. First, move your cursor to the "To:" textbox, single left click on it. Type that e-mail address of the person that you want to send this message to in the textbox. Again, make sure that the e-mail address is correctly spelled, or the message will not be sent at all.

2. Secondly, move your cursor to the "Subject:" textbox and single left click on it. Type a brief summary of what this e-mail is about in the textbox.

3. Thirdly, move your cursor to the blank box on the bottom of the window and single left click on it. Type the actual message in this box.

4. When you are done typing your actual message to this recipient of this message, move your mouse to the send button and single left click on it. Your E-Mail message will then be sent to that e-mail address you inputted.

That is how you put together and send an e-mail message.

Sending Attachments In E-Mails

Attachments are files on your computer that you want to send to people. Pictures, Documents and other files are considered as attachments. Here's how to e-mail documents, spreadsheets, photos or any other type of file.

1. Open your e-mail program, launch a new message window and compose your message.

2. Single left click the **attachment icon** (the paper clip) or insert the file by selecting from the drop-down menu.

3. Browse your hard drive or removable disks to locate the **file** you want to attach. Single left click it to highlight the name, and then click the **Insert** button.

4. An icon or message should now appear indicating that the file has been attached.

51

5. Finally, single left click the **Send** button and off it goes!

That's how you send attachments in E-Mail messages!

Opening E-Mail Messages

When you are at the main screen of Outlook Express/Windows Mail, move your cursor to a specific message on the top part of the program and double left click on the actual message. A pop-up box with the actual message will come up so that you can read the actual message.

Replying To E-Mails

While in that message that is opened in either e-mail program, you will notice a button that says "Reply". Reply Single left click on that button and a window will allow you to type in that same e-mail message what you want to say in response to a particular e-mail. After you have typed in what you wanted to say in response, then single left click the "Send" button. The e-mail will be sent back to the original person who sent the message.

Forwarding E-Mail

While in that message that is opened in and you find that this message would interest someone else that you know, you can send it to them hence the term "Forwarding". you do that by, single left clicking a button that says "Forward" Forward . A window pops up where you can add the e-mail address of the person who you want to send this message to. Insert the e-mail address of the person you want to in the text box and single left click on the "Send" button. This message is now sent to the person.

Deleting E-Mail

On the main screen of the e-mail program, move your cursor to the message you would want to delete and single left click on it. Then move your cursor up to the red "X" in Outlook Express/Windows Mail and single left click on it. The message will now be deleted.

Keeping People & E-Mail Addresses In Your Contact/Address Book

The main reason behind using an address book is to store and maintain information about individuals. After creating entries in an address book, you can use address book to look up information about your personal contacts, such as email addresses and phone numbers.

From the main window in the main window of the Outlook Express/Windows Mail, single left click on the "Addresses" button in Outlook Express or "Contacts" button in Windows Mail. A new contact pop up window will come up. Fill in the information in the textboxes, and single left click on the "OK" button to enter your contact. In Windows Vista® Mail, single left click on the "New Contact" button in the contacts section. Then that will allow you to input all of the information for the person you want to add to your address book. A picture of this pop up windows are shown:

Fill out the information for this person and single left click on the "OK" button. Now that you have a contact in your address book, If you want to send a email to them without typing in their e-mail address all of the time, in the new e-mail window, single left click on the "To" and your address book will come up, find the person in the address book that you want to send the e-mail to and double left click on that name, single left click the "OK" button and then the name will then be placed in the "To" textbox.

Adding Signatures To Your E-Mails

Signatures are comments or information that you could have automatically appear at the bottom of every e-mail so that you don't have to repeatedly type it in. On the Tools menu, single left click Options, single left click on the Signatures tab. The signature menu will come up like the picture shown:

1. To create a signature, single left click the New button and then enter text in the Edit Signature box.

2. Select the Add signatures to all outgoing messages check box.

3. Single left click on the OK button. Now your signature should show at the bottom of every new e-mail you create now.

I hope that this chapter has clarified how to use the most useful features in E-Mail and you can now utilize e-mail for your personal, work or business use.

Chapter Five:

The Critical Task Of Backing Up Your Computer

Chapter Five: The Critical Task of Backing/Restoring Your Computer

Let me begin by saying that doing backups correctly is crucial to being confident that if anything happens to your computer such as a hard drive failure, virus or malware attack, that you don't lose all of your files. Like I had stated about your (C:) drive being like a file cabinet, we can consider a good backup to be like a fireproof safe.

The best way of doing your backups is to use a large flash drive (16GB or Larger) or an external hard drive that you attach to your computer through an usb port. So now you're wondering "How do I start backing up my computer?" Well, are many products at many retail stores that you can buy that does backups, and I tried many of them, but none of them really seemed simple to use, not until I discovered a utility called Fab's Autobackup.

Fab's Autobackup is on the utilities CD. Insert the CD into your CD-ROM Drive by pressing on the eject button on the CD/DVD Rom on the computer. The CD/DVD ROM Drive will eject.

Place the CD/DVD ROM in the drive, label side up and press the eject button again on the CD/DVD ROM to close the drive. The computer will read the CD and then the autoplay menu pops up when the computer recognizes that a CD has been inserted into the computer as shown in the pictures below:

Auto play Feature In Windows Vista® (Windows XP® Has Similar Screen)

Select the "Open Folder To View Files" Menu and a window will pop open to show everything that is on that CD-ROM. Double Left click on the Autobackup and the program will open up a window that looks like the following picture shown:

Like I had said previously in Chapter One is to make sure when you work on your computer is to make sure that you save your files in one of these folders

- My Documents
- My Music
- My Pictures

The reason why it is best for you to save your files, pictures, etc to one of these folders is when you use Autobackup or any other backup program, it backup things from those folders. If things are in other places on the (C:) drive, it is a pretty slim chance your files will be successfully backed up.

To start backing up the computer using Autobackup, attach your external hard drive or flash drive to the computer to one of the usb ports. Opn the Autobackup program by double left clicking on the autobackup icon in the utilities CD. When the Autobackup program starts up, single left click on every box. Then single left click the browse button near the bottom of the screen. A pop up window will come up looking like the picture shown below on the next page:

If you have your flash drive or external hard drive attached to the computer, one of the drives should read Removable Disk (Drive Letter:). Select that drive and click the OK button. Single left click on the backup button. The data is now being backed up to the external hard drive or flash drive. When this process is successful, you have now backed up your computer. Single left click the "Exit" button and the program will close. Not that hard now was it? ☺

Restoring Your Backups

To restore your backups or to transfer them to another computer, plug in the USB flash drive or the external hard drive that you had backed up to in the USB Drive of the computer. Then place the utilities CD-ROM back into the computer and open back up the Fab's Autobackup program. When the main window comes back up, single left click on the "Restore Settings" on the top right part of the window, above the "Current User" section. The Screen will now look like the picture shown below:

Single left click on the "Browse" button at the bottom and the window that asks you what drive to select will come up like the picture shown:

Where your USB external hard drive or flash drive comes up as Removable Drive (Drive Letter:) single left click on the plus symbol to the left of the drive. The contents of the drive will show below when you click on the plus symbol. Autobackup does a beautiful thing when it creates backups. It shows the user that it backed up, also it dates the backup so you know exactly when the backup was done. Single left click on the latest backup folder on the drive and click on the "OK" button. On the main menu, Single left click on the "Restore" Button. All of your documents, settings, etc will be transferred back on the computer. After that has been done, click the "Exit" button and the program will close.

Now that you know how simple it can be to backup and restore your computer, it is very important that you do this exercise at least twice a month, so that you do not lose everything that had been on your computer. There has been countless times where I had to tell people that it was nothing I could do to recover pictures or documents from years past they had stored on the computer when the hard drive totally failed on their computer and would not power up at all.

We are about to move onto the last chapter in this book which will answer a lot of questions I get all of the time from people such as yourself such as "How do I protect my computer from an virus or malware" or "How do I keep my computer running its best" Well, I am about to explain everything in the next chapter "Computer Maintenance and Upkeep"

Chapter Six:

Computer Maintenance And Upkeep

Chapter Six: Computer Maintenance and Upkeep

This is going to be a chapter on what you can do to keep your computer running at optimal performance and put yourself at minimum risk of getting a virus or malware on your computer. When I meet with people for the first time and take a look at their computers, often I see no protection programs installed at all. Listed below are the programs that you HAVE to have installed, ESPECIALLY if this computer is connected to the internet at all.

First, you have to have an antivirus program installed on your computer and update often. This may seem simple, but I have seen computers a lot of times without anything on them or the antivirus program on them is as old as the computer. You have to get a new version of the antivirus program EVERY YEAR! Thousands of viruses are written everyday and released on the internet. If you are not installing a new version of these antivirus programs every year, you are putting yourself at risk of having your computer attacked by a virus.

They are many antivirus programs out there on the market. Examples of anti-virus programs are:

- Norton Antivirus (Part of the Norton 360 Suite) at http://www.symantec.com

- McAfee Antivirus (Part of their Internet Security Suite) at http://www.mcafee.com

But the one I recommend is the AVG antivirus program at http://free.grisoft.com and on the utilities CD. Usually I do not suggest a program that is free, but I used Norton and McAfee over the years and I have found that not only AVG catches more viruses, but AVG does not affect your computers performance. These all-in-one suites don't do a complete job protecting your computer and actually slows down your computer. I find that one program that tries to do everything really is not good at anything. Shown on the next page is what the AVG antivirus program looks like:

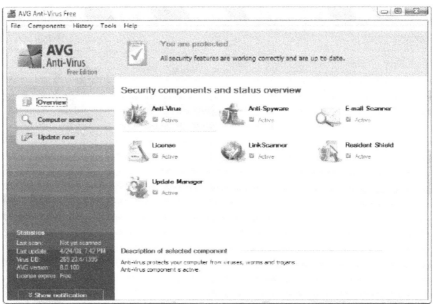

AVG Antivirus Version 8

62

To update AVG, First double left click on the AVG shortcut on your desktop. When the main menu comes up, single left click on the link on the left side of the window that says "Update Now" and the program will check for updates and if there is an update, show a pop-up screen like the one shown in the picture below:

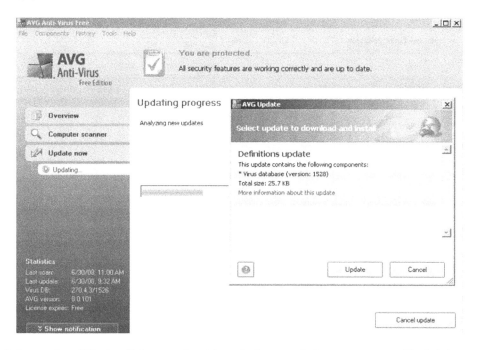

Single left click on the "Update" button in this window and the program will finish updating itself. Simple as that!

You can tryout the other suites mentioned above; everything is a matter of preference. The point that I am trying to make is that you have to install an antivirus program on your computer and update with the newest version EVERY YEAR. Computers are just like a car, you have to keep up with maintenance to keep it running its best!

The second program that I would suggest installing along with the antivirus program and update regularly is an anti-malware scanner of some type. There are programs out there that eliminate spyware such as:

- Ad-Aware at http://www.lavasoft.com/
- Spybot Search And Destroy at http://www.safer-networking.org/en/index.html

I have been using these two programs together for years, but have found a program that does the same thing in one program than with these two called Malware bytes located at http://www.malwarebytes.org/ and on the utilities CD. Shown on the next page is a picture of the main screen of malware bytes:

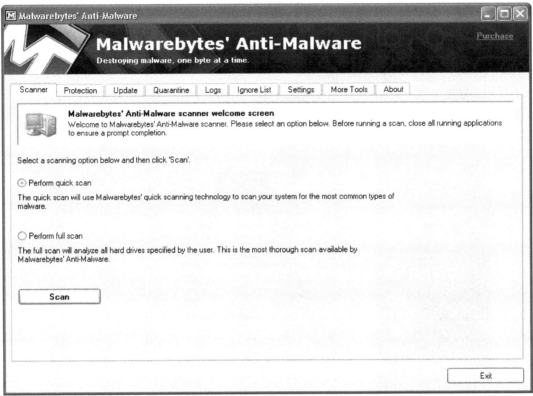

Malware Bytes Anti-Malware Main Screen.

To scan your computer for malware that maybe on your computer, single left click on either "Perform Quick Scan" or "Perform Full Scan" options with your mouse cursor and single left click on the "Scan" button. The program scans your computer for potential problems. To update the malware bytes program, move your mouse cursor to the third tab "Update" on the top and single left click on it. Your screen should look like the picture shown below:

Single left click on the "Check for Updates" button and the program will check for updates and install them if there are any. But these are the two programs you need to have installed on your computer, update and scan your computer in order to effectively keep your computer running at its best. I would talk about installing a firewall, but Microsoft already has a firewall installed for both Windows XP® and Vista. Also your internet router also has a firewall installed on it. There is no need to add another firewall onto your computer and risk slowing your internet and computer down.

I almost forgot to make this point – The most crucial thing you can do to not to have problems with your computer is NOT TO USE FREE MUSIC DOWNLOADING PROGRAMS SUCH AS LIMEWIRE, KAZAA OR FROSTWIRE!!!! Viruses and Malware live on these sites and are the fastest ways that you can get your computer infected. You can buy your music very cheaply through http://www.amazon.com or at iTunes at http://www.Apple.com/itunes/. Lately on the news (MSNBC) , hackers have successfully exploited the program to scan computers hard drives and to gain access to peoples tax return information among other things. The story starts on the next page:

P2P networks threaten home PC security
Media-sharing software loaded by kids can expose trove of financial data

Tami Olson's oldest daughter exposed the family's financial records online when she installed a popular music-sharing software package.

By Jeremy Brilliant and Holly Stephen
NBC News

INDIANAPOLIS - Users of peer-to-peer platforms, also known as P2P networks, may be under attack from entertainment lawyers policing copyright violations, but they can also be an easy target for identity thieves. And they may never know about it if it's their kids who load the software.

Take the Olsons, a typical Indiana family: Christopher and Tami have three daughters, as well as a family dog.

The dog's name can't yet be found online, but everyone else's can, thanks to security holes in popular P2P music downloading software. So can their birthdates and the family's income and banking information.

"Unbelievable ... how did it get out there?" asked Tami Olson, who pays bills and does her taxes online.

The Olsons' private data were found through LimeWire, a software program used to download music and videos. Within a matter of minutes, two of the Olsons' tax returns were available.

"Well, this is our entire tax history. It's going to have, I imagine, the Social Security number of my husband, myself and our three children right there," Tami Olson said.

She was right. In addition to the family's income, the data included banking and routing numbers.

With the expansion of broadband service making it easier to share large media files, more than 60 million Americans have downloaded and used P2P services like LimeWire and Kazaa, according to the Federal Trade Commission and the Electronic Frontier Foundation, a digital-rights group.

The Olsons' oldest daughter unknowingly exposed the family's personal and financial records after downloading LimeWire. "She didn't really think there was anything wrong with that," her mother said. "I told them to get it off immediately because I have a lot of personal info out there."

Total exposure
Many users don't realize that when they use file-sharing software, they are putting their hard drives on the network, to be shared with anyone else using the network.

Users can specify what files are private, but many don't, said Eugene Spafford, a computer science professor at Purdue University and executive director of the Center for Education and Research in Information Assurance and Security.

"One problem with peer-to-peer is getting the settings wrong and sharing your entire disk or your entire personal file system, rather than simply the files you think you're sharing," Spafford said.

"We've created a culture and an expectation that you just install the software and you never bother to read that license that comes up or the warnings that come up," he said.

Spafford said the Olsons' story was not unique.

"Parents don't understand the technology well enough to talk to their kids," he said. Security experts say it's easy to exploit such vulnerabilities because data can be found through simple search strings, like "[bank name] July statement" or "[bank name] routing information."

'Giving criminals the keys to your computer'
Just this month, a Seattle man was charged with identity theft in a case that illustrates just how glaring such vulnerabilities are.

The man, Gregory Kopiloff, used LimeWire, the same software used by the Olsons, to dig into hundreds of hard drives, prosecutors said. He was accused of harvesting tax returns and student aid forms from at least 83 people and buying $73,000 in merchandise through fake credit card accounts he set up using the data.

Investigators said most of the victims had teenage children and did not know the software was even on their computers.

"If you are running file-sharing software, you are giving criminals the keys to your computer," Assistant U.S. Attorney Kathryn Warma said. "Criminals are getting access to incredibly valuable information."

Not fully understanding the P2P risks can also open the door for others to use your hard drive to hide evidence of their own crimes.

"If you've got a Machine, do you know what's in every directory on your Machine?" Spafford asked. "Probably not.

"These criminals will take those Machines and store the contraband material on them, because they know if a warrant is served on their home and they're found with that on their disk, they can be prosecuted."

Getting hit with the news that you're a victim of identity theft is becoming more common. The Federal Trade Commission says as many as 9 million Americans' identities are stolen every year. So how do you protect your computer files from P2P identity theft? Know what's installed on your computer, and take the time to look at the security settings. Tami Olson said she had learned the lesson.

"Obviously, I'm going to be more careful about what I store in my computer," she said. "If my kids are going to download in the future, I want to be there. I want to read what they're downloading."

Chapter Seven:

Taking Back Control Of Your Computer

Chapter Seven: Taking Back Control of Your Computer

Over the years, many people, especially parents that have computer savvy children asked me that if anything could be installed on their computer to monitor and have more control over what their children can or cannot do on the family computer, and on the Internet at home. And up to that point, there was no simplistic or easy way to do so.

There are some products out on the market such as net nanny that monitored what users see on the Internet, but they sort of worked to varying degrees. But there was no way of controlling what users do to the computer itself outside the Windows user account settings, so the owners of computers were still having issues with other people downloading illegal music sharing programs, viruses, malware and other programs onto their computer.

Microsoft must have listened to these frustrations from users of Windows, especially parents of children who really wanted to know what their children were doing on their home computers. So they have implemented the new Family Live Safety Suite which allows parents to:

* Set up web filtering to allow only the content you want your kids to see. Use contact management to choose who they talk to online when they use Windows Live Messenger, Windows Live Hotmail, and Windows Live Spaces. You can customize settings for each family member.

* Manage your kids' safety settings from any computer, and get Web-based reports that show what your kids are doing online. You can grant or deny requests to view specific Web sites from almost any computer online.

* Steer your kids toward appropriate websites. Also set time limits that you desire your children to be able to use the computer

In this chapter, we will go over in detail how to utilize these powerful features to take back control of your computer! To get started using these great features, you need to first go to the Microsoft's Windows Essentials Website, which is located at http://download.live.com/familysafety or insert the Reg's Practical Guide Utilities CD to download and install the Microsoft Live Essentials programs which includes the Family Safety filter you need to have installed on your computer to be able to move forward in this chapter.

To take back control of your computer, you need to understand that they are three phases to taking back control of your computer. I will go step by step into the individual phases:

The First Phase:

The first phase of taking back control of your computer consists of setting time limits on when certain users are allowed to use the computer at all. Microsoft has added enhanced user controls to Windows 7 for you to be able to set specified hours for other users outside of yourself to use the computer.

To enable the settings to limit computer time, First move your mouse cursor to the Start menu and single left click on it. Move your mouse cursor to the control panel option and single left click on it. The control panel should come up like the picture shown below:

Move your mouse cursor to the "User Accounts and Family Safety" link and single left click on it. The next screen should look like the picture shown below:

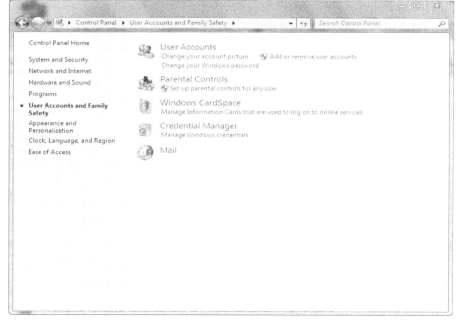

Move your mouse cursor and Single left click on the "User Accounts" link. The settings for the current user should come up in the next screen. More than likely, it is another user account that you have setup that you would want to monitor, so you would have to tell Windows to set controls on another account.

So what you will do is move your mouse cursor over to the "Manage Another Account" link in that window and single left click on it. The window should look like the following picture shown below:

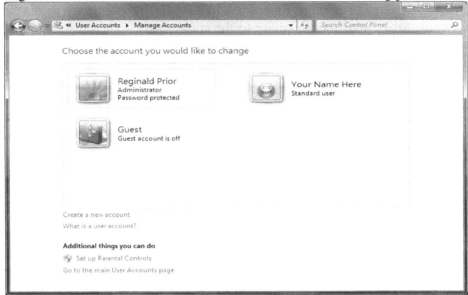

Note – If you haven't created a separate user account for a user other than yourself, it would be a good idea to go back to chapter two and read the section "Adding/Changing Users In Windows" to add a separate account for that user.

The user that I want to set the restrictions for in this case is the account that I had created on this computer named "Your Name Here". So move my mouse to that account icon and single left click on that account. The detailed user account information window should come up like the window shown below:

Move your mouse cursor to the "Set up Parental Controls" link and single left click on it. The parental controls main menu will come up like the picture shown below:

Move your mouse cursor to the account that you want to enforce the time settings on and single left click on it. The parental settings main menu window for this particular account should come up looking like the window shown below:

In this window, you should see a link called "Time Limits". Move your mouse cursor to that link and single left click on it. In this window, you would use your mouse and single left click to block out the times that this user is not to be signed onto the computer.

In the last window, I have limited the computer usage time for the user "Your Name Here" to be able to use the computer Monday thru Friday from 3PM to 7PM and on the weekends from 6AM to 10PM. You can set the time limits to your satisfaction and single left click on the "OK" button to save the desired usage time for that particular user. This takes care of phase one of taking back control of your computer. We now move on to the Second Phase – Restricting use of computer software.

The Second Phase:

You might be asking yourself "Why would I suggest limiting the programs on the computer that other users can use?" The answer is pretty simple. Many people who are trying to get around restrictions on a computer usually would download and install or use other programs on the computer to try to get around the restrictions. And if you limit the programs that they can use to get around the restrictions, the better and safer your computer would be.

On the parental settings main menu window, move your mouse cursor over to and single left click on the "Allow and Block Specific Programs" link. A window will come up and ask you if this user is allowed to use all of the programs on the computer (Not Recommended) or Use the programs that I allow.

Single left click on the choice where it says that the user can only use the programs I allow. The computer will then scan for programs that are currently installed on this computer, and show them in this list. Most users usually only use three programs on the computer. Examples of those programs can be:

1. E-Mail
2. Internet Browsing
3. Word Processing (Typing Documents In Microsoft Word)

Everything else on the computer is not necessary for other users to access to operate the computer. The more programs other users have access to, the more likely that they can find loopholes in these programs to do other things to the computer. So what you would do in this window is scroll through this list and move your mouse cursor to the checkboxes on the left of the programs that allows users to do the tasks listed above and single left click on the checkbox to allow them to use that program. Everything else can be left unchecked.

When you are done tweaking these settings, move your mouse cursor to the "OK" button and single left click on it. You will return to the parental settings main menu window.

The Third And Final Phase:

The final and most important phase of taking back control of your computer is limiting the access to websites. The internet is a great tool for doing many things such as research among other things. But it is also a place where bad things can happen also. Like I explained in chapter six, Identity theft is the fastest growing crime and it is not getting better any time soon.

Programs like Frostwire, Limewire shares files between computers on the Internet can put you at risk for identity theft, viruses and other things. The best way to protect yourself this is to limit users from going to those websites to download and install the programs in the first place. And parents of children does not want their children being exposed to things that are freely on the Internet such as dating websites, pornographic material among other things.

Like I had stated at the beginning of this chapter, Microsoft has implemented in Windows 7 the new Family Live Safety Suite. This allows you not only to limit the access to certain websites, you can track other activity that the user is doing on the computer itself such as which programs are being used on the computer and if they are downloading files and other things.

You implement changes in the Live Family Suite by the parental settings main menu of the account you want to put restrictions on, move your mouse cursor over to the Windows Live Family Safety Link and single left click on it. Since this is the first time that you are setting up restrictions on this account, A log in window will come up like the picture shown on the next page asking you to sign up for the Windows Live Website.

You would need to sign up for this free service. This website allows you to change settings from any computer on the Internet and also view activity reports at any time. Also your other users can request access to certain websites which you can approve or deny from this service.

Move your mouse cursor over to the blue "Sign Up" link to be redirected to the Windows live website to sign up for this free service. The webpage would look like the picture shown on the next page:

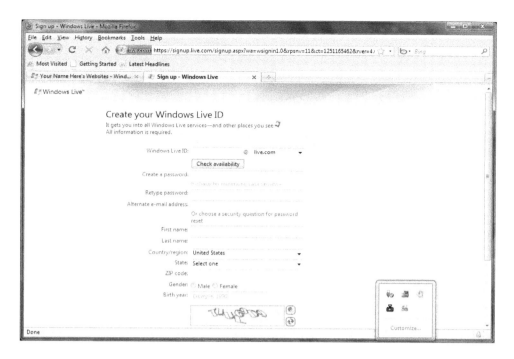

After you have signed up for the Windows Live Service, You can go back to the family safety sign in window as shown in the picture below, and enter in the textboxes the e-mail address and the password that you entered for signing up for the service and move your mouse cursor and single left clicking on the "Sign In" button.

The main screen that allows you to restrict websites that users can view looks like the picture on the next page:

Note – After you have setup everything on the computer for the first time, you can go on any computer that is connected to the Internet and point the web browser to http://fss.live.com/ and use your username and password to sign into the website and make changes and view all activity on demand.

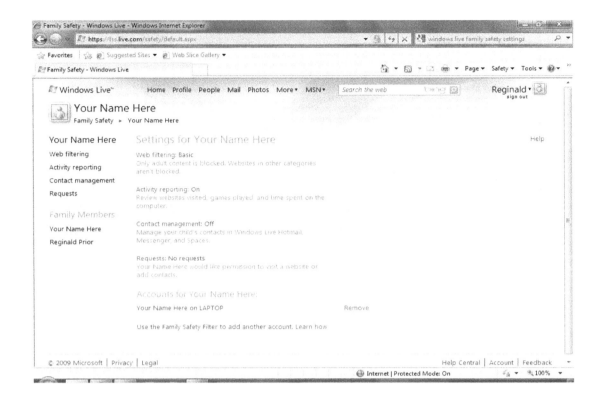

As you can see on the main page for Windows Live Family Safety website, you have four sections on where you can customize how and what you want to have monitored for each user that is on the family computer. Here's a short overview about which each section does to protect your computer.

Web Filtering – Web filtering allows you to control what content is delivered over the <u>Web</u>. This puts you totally in charge about which websites other users are allowed to see. To enable a web filter for a specific user, first move your mouse cursor to the user under the "Family Members" section of the webpage and single left click on it. Secondly, move your mouse cursor to the "Web Filtering" link and single left click on it. The webpage should look like the picture shown on the next page:

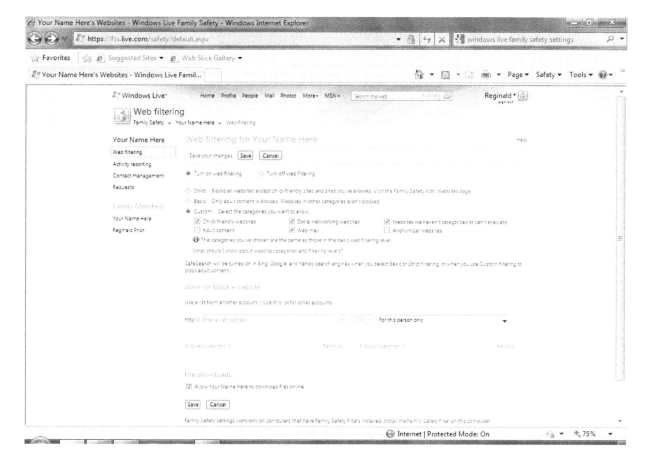

There are three ways that you can set up web filtering:

Strict (Not Recommended) – This setting really blocks just about every webpage except ones that Microsoft has deemed Kid Friendly. This list is located at http://fss.live.com/kids/

Basic – This setting blocks all adult content, but allows many other types of websites such as social networking (myspace.com, facebook.com, twitter.com)

Custom – This setting allows you to customize filtering by which types of websites other users are allowed to see or not to see.

My suggestion is to set the filtering to the Basic level and under the "Allow or Block a Website" manually type in a webpage that you don't want your other users to visit. You can tweak around with the settings in this section until you get the desired filters for the other users on this computer. When you are done with setting up web filtering, move your mouse cursor to the "Save" button and single left click on it. Your web filtering settings will be saved and implemented on the computer the next time that user signs into the computer.

Activity Reporting – View reports on computer activities for each user. You would know if other users are trying to hack the computer or get around the restrictions that you have set on the computer at a moments notice. The Activity Reporting screen looks like the picture shown below:

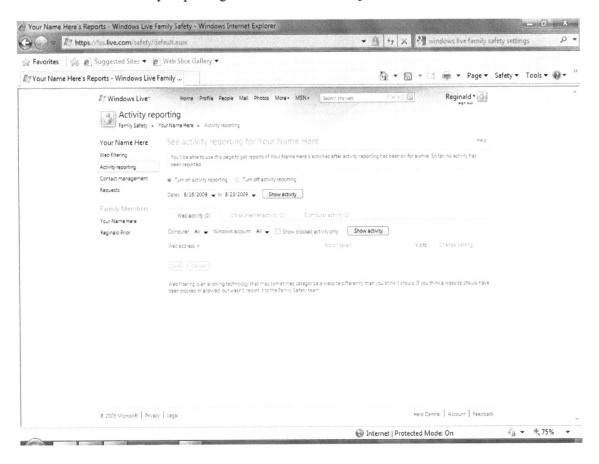

Contact Management – Contact Management helps you know who your kids are talking to in e-mail or blogs on Windows Live Spaces, or in IM on Windows Live Messenger. Contact management allows you to approve or reject each new contact. The contact management screen looks like the picture shown on the next page:

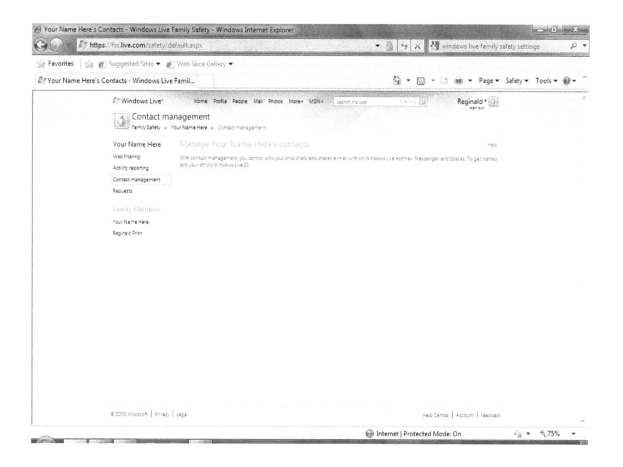

Requests – Your users can request access to blocked websites by clicking on a link to send you an e-mail so that you can research the requested website before allowing or denying access to it. The picture shown below shows what a blocked website would look like on the users screen and how they would submit a request to you to unblock the website.

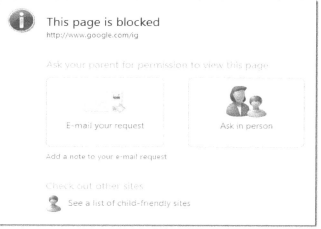

When the user requests access to a particular webpage, it will look like the following picture under the Windows Live Family Safety requests page:

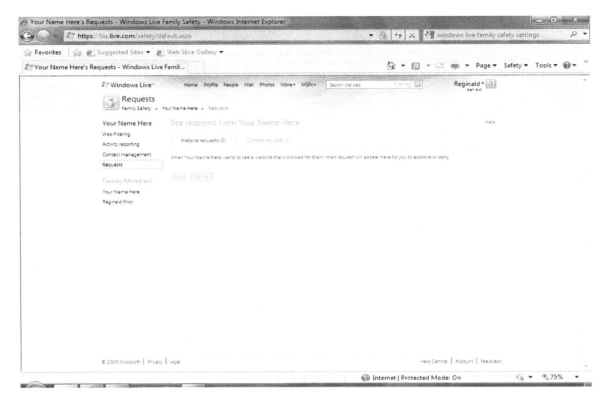

In this section, you will see all of the webpage requests from all of the users on your computer, you have the option now to allow access to that webpage or deny access to that website. This allows you as the administrator to investigate this webpage to make sure that it is a webpage that is acceptable to you and accept or deny the request as you see fit.

I hope that you have gained a lot of knowledge in learning more about your computer by reading this book. Just like in the preface, you are the most important critic and value all of your feedback about this book so that I can improve future texts. Thank you for reading and look forward to hearing from you!!

Works Cited

Jeremy Brilliant and Holly Stephen.
"P2P networks threaten home PC security."

MSNBC Online. 18 October 2007.
http://www.msnbc.msn.com/id/21364575/
3/17/2009

Notes

Notes

www.ingramcontent.com/pod-product-compliance
Lightning Source LLC
Chambersburg PA
CBHW060457060326
40689CB00020B/4556